United States
Department of
Agriculture

Forest Service

Southern
Research Station

General Technical
Report SRS–155

In Land of Cypress and Pine: An Environmental History of the Santee Experimental Forest, 1683-1937

Hayden R. Smith

Author:

Hayden R. Smith, Ph.D. Candidate, The University
of Georgia, Department of History, Athens, GA 30602.

Cover
Limerick Plantation, 1916. Note: Live Oak drive in foreground. Photograph
by W.B. Barrows, courtesy of the Forest History Society, Durham, NC; USFS
negative number 26336A.

May 2012

Southern Research Station
200 W. T. Weaver Blvd.
Asheville, NC 28804

www.srs.fs.usda.gov

In Land of Cypress and Pine: An Environmental History of the Santee Experimental Forest, 1683-1937

Hayden R. Smith

ABSTRACT

The Santee Experimental Forest is a 6,100-acre research facility located within the Francis Marion National Forest, SC. Situated within the Huger Creek watershed in the headwaters of the East Branch of the Cooper River, the Santee Experimental Forest supports research in forest ecology, silviculture, prescribed fire, forest hydrology, ecosystem restoration, and wildlife management. Although the Santee Experimental Forest came into existence based on early 20th-century timber practices and the resulting needs for information on sustainable forestry practices, its boundaries have supported a wide array of human development for over 300 years. This paper provides an overarching history of land use on the Forest and regional perspectives. This environmental history also explains how Huger Creek ecosystems influenced people's alteration the landscape. Livestock, naval stores, rice, cotton, and truck farming represent human production on the land from the colonial to postbellum eras. Logging and forest management replaced the earlier industries as political, social, and economic factors evolved at the turn of the 20th century. By documenting human development upon the land, a clear understanding of changing landscapes and ecological succession provides needed context for the Santee Experimental Forest's scope and mission. This environmental history also provides the basis for considering the influences of past uses on the delivery of ecosystem goods and services in a restored forest landscape.

Keywords: Environmental history, forest history, forest succession, Limerick Plantation, rice culture, Windsor Plantation.

Foreword

Rich in resources like swamps and freshwater tidal creeks, the southeastern coastal plain has always attracted human settlement, starting with Native Americans in prehistoric times. By the 18th and 19th centuries, a mosaic of uses marked the landscape. Settlers converted forested swamps to rice cultivation and used uplands for crops, naval store products, lumber, and grazing. In 1937, as agriculture waned and forest growth rebounded, the Forest Service, U.S. Department of Agriculture, established the Santee Experimental Forest to provide information needed to restore and manage these forested lands. Over the past 75 years, research on pine and hardwood silviculture, prescribed fire, and wildlife management has been instrumental to developing approaches to ensure forest sustainability. Today, that legacy continues with the Santee Experimental Forest providing research essential to resolving some of the most pressing environmental issues facing today's rapidly urbanizing southeastern Atlantic coastal plain.

Missing from this research is an appreciation for historical context. Ecological perspectives derived from research on the Santee Experimental Forest are best understood if based on the long and complex history of agriculture and exploitive lumbering that dates back to the early 1700s. This legacy of agricultural use, which continued into the 20th century, is still evident on more recently forested land; however, until the advent of new remote sensing data, the extent of this legacy wasn't known. The area's environmental history continues to affect ecological processes, albeit in ways we're only now beginning to understand. Conversely, the dynamic and productive forests of today demonstrate an incredible resilience. These evolving conditions make the Santee Experimental Forest vital in its role as a reference forest landscape to the rapidly changing urban and suburban landscape of the south Atlantic coastal plain.

This publication provides a significant introduction to the environmental history of the Santee Experimental Forest, and it will serve as a foundation for better understanding today's coastal forested landscape. Over the last three centuries, the lands that make up the Santee Experimental Forest have gone from minimally disturbed forests to intensively worked lands to managed forests. Understanding the environmental implications associated with that history provides insights into the historical uses as well as the contemporary ecosystems of the forest today. In the 1800s, freshwater tidal creeks attracted the plantation development; today, these tidal creeks provide an opportunity to study how sea level rise may affect ecological processes.

Environmental history is the basis for linking different stages of landscape development across the centuries. It also is a way to better understand that what we perceive as "natural" in the landscape is actually part of an ongoing evolution of how people interact with the natural world. And the better our understanding of that process, the more likely we are to manage our resources wisely.

Carl C. Trettin
Team Leader, Center for Forested Wetlands Research
U.S. Department of Agriculture, Forest Service
Southern Research Station
Cordesville, SC

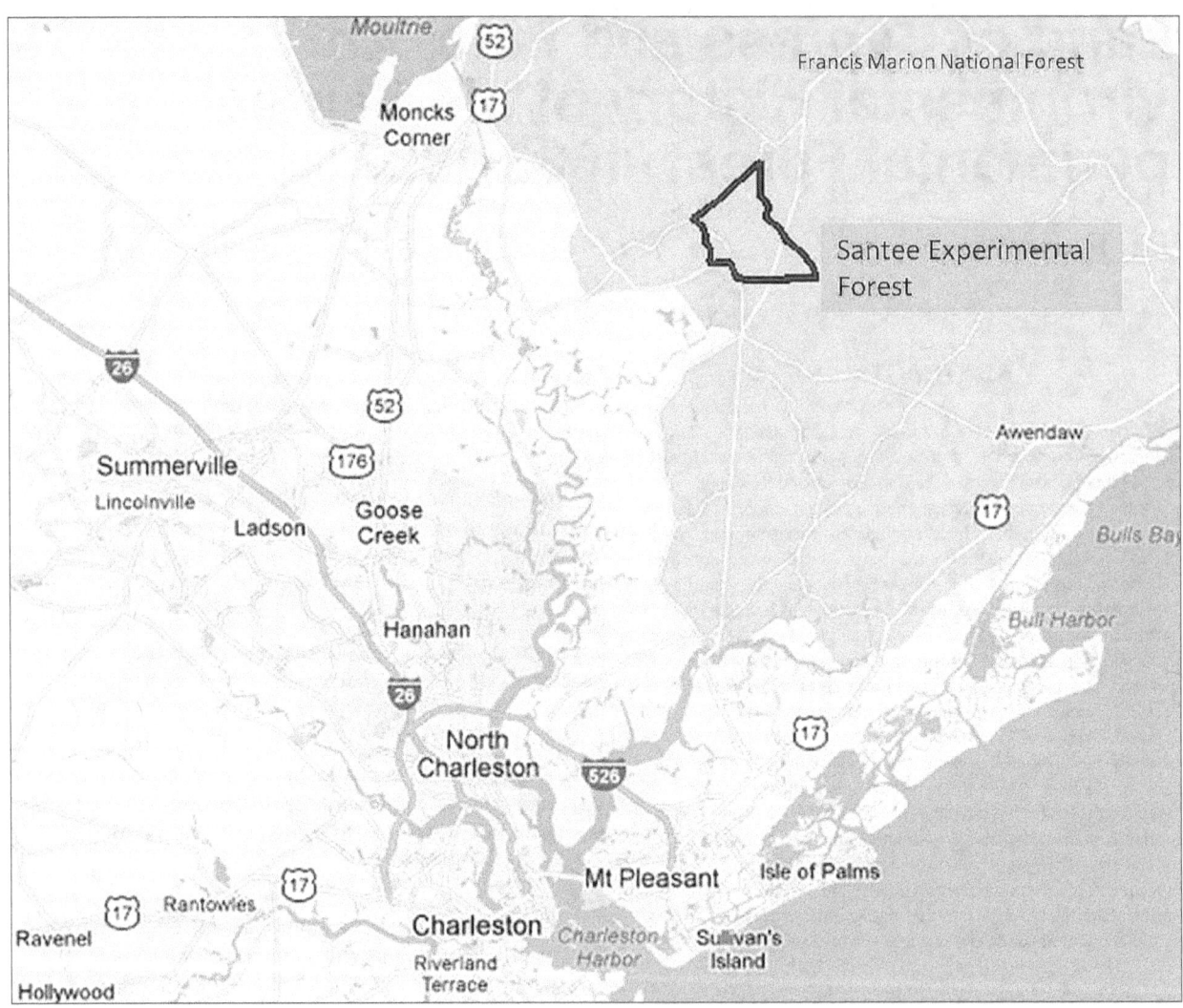

Figure 1—Location of the Santee Experimental Forest in the Francis Marion National Forest; located in Berkeley County, outside of Charleston, SC. (Data source: http://cybergis.uncc.edu/santee/searchf.php Web GIS portal of Santee Experimental Forest Land Resource Data. Prepared by Lee Moreland)

Introduction

In 1779, Alexander Hewatt published a narrative history of colonial South Carolina. In the sweeping overview of political, military, and economic developments shaping the colony, Hewatt devotes a chapter to the agricultural development of the Lowcountry cash crops, explaining that topography played an important foundation in the colony's land use history.[1] "Nature points out to [the planter] where to begin his labours," Hewatt writes, "for the soil, however various, is everywhere easily distinguished, by the different kinds of trees which grow upon it." The Santee Experimental Forest spans three centuries of Hewatt's connection between people and the environment (Hewatt 1779).

Located on the Huger Creek watershed, the landscape Hewatt describes directly contributed to the South Carolina Lowcountry's distinctive agricultural history (fig. 1). Rice, cotton, and indigo were three cash crops that fueled South Carolina's plantation enterprise. After the Civil War, timber became the region's central commodity.

The foundation of South Carolina's Lowcountry agricultural history is the watershed's topography. High land ridges and low-lying wetlands provided zones where the plantations of Huger Creek profited from successful agricultural endeavors, and where timber stands attracted logging industries in the 20th century. The history of the 6,100-acre Santee Experimental Forest is also a story of how the natural landscape shaped people's lives, because topography dictated settlement patterns and commercial pursuits. How the region's residents—both free and enslaved—related with the environment contributed to a broader story of social and cultural identity in the South Carolina Lowcountry and the Southeastern Coastal Plain.

---

[1] The South Carolina lowcountry (or Lowcountry) is both a geographical and cultural region, defined in this paper as the Outer Coastal Plain and Coastal Zone. The South Carolina Lowcountry extends the length of the coast and inland approximately 50 miles.

This report presents the history of land use on three centrally located plantations and three marginal plantations within what are now the Santee Experimental Forest boundaries. Colonial settlement in this area began in 1683. English and French Huguenot colonists established rural settlements in the upland pine stands, while slaves provided labor for the agricultural ventures of the colonists. The cultivation of crops took hold by the beginning of the 18th century, with slaves carving out miles of embankments and canals to successfully irrigate the crop. By the 19th century, rice farming influenced almost every aspect of life along South Carolina's Coastal Plain, with the cash crop providing a foundation for the region's economic success, social hierarchy, and unique cultural formation.

Huger Creek residents faced new social and economic decisions in the post-emancipation era. Former slaves restructured their lives, encountering the joys and challenges of newfound freedom. African-American residents grappled with whether to continue pursuing a livelihood in rice farming or to embark on new economic and agricultural courses. Former plantation owners, on the other hand, struggled to keep up with rapidly changing markets. Huger Creek property owners initially maintained cotton and rice farming, but they eventually sold their plantations to timber companies. Timber harvesting changed the spatial landscape once again, as logging moved land use away from rice and cotton fields and into timber stands. This report documents 50 years of the timber industry's impact on the region, and describes subsequent events that led to the Santee Experimental Forest's creation in 1937.

Cypress Barony and Early Plantation Agriculture

Barony Development

The current political boundary of the Santee Experimental Forest overlaps the northeastern half of the colonial Cypress Barony. The barony was a 12,000-acre tract that the Lord Proprietors granted to Landgrave Thomas Colleton in August 1683. The Lord Proprietors—eight English nobility who served as the ruling landlords of the proprietary colony—gave these baronies as rewards to English and Barbadian gentry, who in turn managed the landed estates like old-world feudal estates. Thomas Colleton was the second son of Sir John Colleton, one of original Lord Proprietors of Carolina. The elder Colleton supported Charles I's unsuccessful campaign to maintain the Crown during the English Civil War. The overthrow of Charles I in 1648 forced Colleton to flee England for Barbados, where he developed large and profitable sugar estates. Upon Charles II's rise to power in 1660, Colleton was rewarded as one of eight proprietors to the newly established Carolina (Dunn 1972, Weir 1997).

Cypress Barony land use represented the agro-economic experimentation occurring upon these large tracts during the late 17th century. Planters experimented with a variety of enterprises that reflected economic demands of the time. Furs, cattle, naval stores, provisional crops, timber, rice, and indigo were all popular commodities during the colonial period. Thomas Colleton was an absentee owner living in Barbados, so he depended upon Elias Horry to manage Cypress Barony. Horry, a French Huguenot, owned Hampton Plantation on the Santee River but oversaw the enslaved laborers living on highland settlement later called Limerick Plantation. In comparison, Thomas' brother, Governor James Colleton, grew rice, barley, wheat, peas, cotton, indigo, and Indian corn on his Wadboo Barony approximately 8 miles northwest of Cypress Barony. James's overseer, John Stewart, most notably experimented with rice cultivation, along with cotton and silkworm production (Lees 1981).

Cattle Ranching

Of the diverse agro-economic experimentation, cattle ranching became the most profitable enterprise in Cypress Barony at the turn of the 18th century. Ranching required relatively little labor and capital as colonists practiced free-range livestock throughout the undeveloped plantation landscape. Hogs and cattle foraged freely in the woods and savannahs throughout the summer while migrating down to the marshland canebrakes during the winter. Savannahs were open grassland and shrub breaks within larger longleaf pine (*Pinus palustris*) or cypress-hardwood communities. To improve savannahs by removing encroaching plant species, Carolinians adopted the Native American custom of burning woodlands during the winter.[2] Colonists sought to satisfy the demand in New England, Jamaica, and Barbados for salted beef and pork. By 1682, meat products were the most profitable exports in the colony. As herds increased in numbers, greater demand for slaves to tend to the cattle also increased. When Peter Colleton sold Cypress Barony in 1707, he advertised 800 head of cattle and 15 slaves living on the property. Contrary to Colleton's advertisement, cattle hunter Peter Herrington stated in a 1708 deposition that he could find "noe more cattle then the Number of four hundred & Sixty head both great & small & that there were never was more to his knowledge and during his time of Imployment on the sd. Barony then the Number of five hundred and fourty head of cattle brought in one year" (Lees 1981).

By 1708, at least 1,000 of the 1,800 slaves in South Carolina tended to cattle. Roaming to forage for food, the cattle grazed throughout the tidal marshes, upland

---

[2] This practice was an example of human manipulation of naturally occurring forces that led to the evolution of fire resistant communities and the development of distinct ecosystems relying on fire. For more information on fire and culture, see Pyne (1997).

3

savannahs, and bottomland stream floodplains. Whereas the European settlers might have had little reason to venture into less desirable landscapes, slaves were forced to navigate through these landscapes to round up livestock, thus familiarizing themselves with the subtly changing ecosystems. A writer in 1708 observed of the "1000 good Negroes that knows the Swamps and Woods, most of them [are] Cattle-hunters." Slaves served as the "middling" between plantations and wilderness, while planters attempted to define boundaries between the two spatial environments. Their everyday exposure to the environment, combined with individual knowledge of land use, enabled these enslaved people to creatively envision how to put the landscape to work for their own benefit. Whether actively herding animals for their enslavers or temporarily escaping into the wilderness for a brief reprieve, these early cattle-hands served as a conduit between the desirable and undesirable landscape (Edelson 2006b, Otto 1987, Ver Steeg 1975, Weir 1997).

Peter Colleton sold Cypress Barony to Barbadian merchants John Gough, Dominick Arthur, and Michael Mahon on July 18, 1707. The Lord Proprietors approved Colleton's sale on April 14, 1709, as the fundamental constitutions of Carolina—the legal foundation of the proprietary colony—prevented Landgraves from selling property outside of bloodlines after 1701. Colleton divided the barony into three divisions, where Gough and Mahon purchased 3,500 acres apiece, and Arthur purchased 5,000 acres. The Santee Experimental Forest would later exist on the Mahon and Arthur divisions (Smith 1911).

Colleton's division of Cypress Barony created lasting political boundaries that would define plantation borders. Gough's property would become Kensington, Hyde Park, and St. James Plantations. Mahon's parcel became Limerick plantation. Arthur's portion became Limerick, Nicholson, Windsor, Fishbrook, and Silk Hope Plantations. Upon receiving these proprietary land grants, Gough, Mahon, and Arthur immigrated to Carolina from Barbados. Mahon named his division "Lymerick" after his native Irish town but devoted only 4 years to Limerick's plantation enterprise. By 1713, he sold 3,415 of the original 3,500 proprietary acres to Daniel Huger (II) and subsequently returned to Barbados. Judging from the £800 price, Mahon had not established a definitive economy from Limerick's landscape. While Mahon acquired "planter" status by the land transaction, more than likely his agricultural endeavors consisted of agricultural experimentation, cattle ranching, and timber harvesting (Lees 1981, Smith 1911).

Naval Stores

Naval stores provided additional revenue during the first three decades of the 18th century. Pinelands led colonists to extract tar and pitch, while the pine and mixed hardwood forests provided timber. Shipbuilders adhered pitch to caulk ship hulls, while turpentine served as a varnish and paint thinner. Tar provided a wood preservative, rigging protection, and deck coating. England imported tar and pitch from Baltic countries during the 17th century, but rising prices from the Stockholm Tar Company and diminishing supply during Sweden's war with Russia (1699-1721) motivated the English Parliament to pass the bounty act of 1705. The bounty encouraged colonial production tar and pitch, turpentine, rosin, hemp, and lumber (Weir 1997).

By the second decade of the 18th century, naval stores became the central commodity for South Carolina. In 1718, exports from South Carolina to Great Britain included 27,660 barrels of tar and 18,414 barrels of pitch, plus additional imports to the West Indies of 5,677 barrels of tar and 4,187 barrels of pitch. However, parliament terminated the bounty in 1724, resulting in depressed prices. Sweden's higher quality of tar and pitch lessened the demand of Carolina production, where global economic demand shifted to the Baltic methods after the 1724 bounty expired. By 1731, shipments dropped to 2,063 barrels of tar and 10,754 barrels of pitch. Exports further declined by 1748, to 5,521 barrels of pitch (Gray 1933).

The Southern forest's prime longleaf ecosystem created a desirable landscape for naval store entrepreneurs. The longleaf pine has a high resin content compared to the New England white pine (*Pinus strobus*), so Southern colonists could extract higher yields. Colonists dotted the forest with tar kilns, stacking pine trees a story high and igniting the timber to burn out the tar. A pipe at the bottom of the kiln would funnel the tar away from the fire and collected in a barrel. They would dig shallow depressions and line them with clay, which would form a saucer to collect extracted tar. Colonists placed tar kilns in between navigable waterways and bountiful pine stands. A barrel of tar consisted of 31.5 gallons and eight barrels could weigh up to a ton, so waterways were ideal for shipping this heavy commodity. Tar kilns located on the northwest corner of Limerick plantation provide an example of the spatial boundaries between forest and river. The 18th-century site existed on the sandy highlands adjacent to Little Hell Hole Swamp and the public road. From this location, enslaved laborers transported barrels to Limerick Plantation's landing, shipped by boat down the East Branch of the Cooper River to Charles Town (Hart 1986, Weir 1997).

African Diaspora and Inland Rice Cultivation

Inland rice cultivation resulted in the first significant plantation development in colonial South Carolina. Productive inland rice cultivation led to massive rural development and increasing demand for backcountry infrastructure. The successful rice economy also led to increasing demand for labor that fueled the trans-Atlantic slave trade and African diaspora in South Carolina. Inland rice plantations, in turn, provided an economic foundation in the Lowcountry. Charles Town became the central trading destination and South Carolina became a model mercantilist colony. The accumulation of capital helped induce the colony's economic expansion, which was seen in society, religion, and government. Inland plantations became a landscape where people, influenced by the dramatic cultural, political, and economic currents occurring throughout the Atlantic world, constructed distinctive identities that still exist today. European, African, Caribbean, and Native American customs played out in plantation labor, architecture, food ways, language, and religion. Finally, inland rice culture led to the development of the task system. This method of controlling enslaved people allowed planters or overseers to enforce work in the fields until specific assignments, or tasks, were finished on a daily basis. This system was unique to Lowcountry rice plantations, and it provided slaves some freedom to tend to subsistence needs, yet gave planters less responsibility to maintain basic care for their laborers (Morgan 1998).

Providence Rice Culture

Limerick, Windsor, and Fishbrook's plantation economy and social formation took a dramatic shift with the introduction of rice cultivation in the early 18th century. Early Carolinians originally grew rice in a "providence" style on savannahs and small-stream floodplains. This method resembled typical English farming practices of tilling the soil and broadcasting seeds, where the crop then depended on the dampness of the soil from rainwater or freshets. Freshets occurred when storms or hurricanes provided more rain than the soil could absorb and streams could channel, causing "rapid torrents" that were "sudden and violent" as they flowed downhill (Catesby 1977). Colonists, however, experienced difficulties cultivating rice in the providence style. Planters could not plow the land as they would in England because stumps and roots hindered initial tilling. Also, early rice planters encountered competition with unwanted vegetation suffocating the crop from sunlight and nutrients. Without methods to eradicate weeds, through flooding and weeding, the providence practice became, to some, "more drudgery and charge than it was all worth" (Stewart 1931).

Colonists originally saw swamps and low-lying areas as "wastelands." Early colonialists saw wooded wetlands as evil or "dismal" because the dense, impenetrable landscape challenged their norms of orderliness and presented an incomprehensible, chaotic landscape. Also, malaria and other diseases carried by the *Anopheles* mosquito took their toll on people living near wetlands during the summer months. The flat and narrow watercourses—in Fox Gully, a tributary of Turkey Creek—were located above tidal influenced rivers and received water runoff from higher elevations to form creeks and streams flowing into the Cooper River and surrounding tributaries. The small-stream floodplains were "dominated by swamp trees with a herbaceous ground cover or cane-breaks." Soil permeability dictated the dominant tree species of black gum (*Nyssa sylvatica*), sweet gum (*Liquidambar styraciflua*), live oak (*Quercus virginiana*), red maple (*Acer rubrum*), and longleaf pine *(P. palustris)* (Porcher, in press).

Although colonists first experimented with growing rice on open upland fields in the late 17th century, the grain also represented a component of the Afro-Caribbean culture transferred from Barbados to South Carolina. Rice was a central part of West African culture before colonial contact. As the slave trade connected West African ports to Barbados, slaves simultaneously transferred their cultural identity to the New World. Once slaves came to the New World to work on South Carolina plantations, they brought their cultural, social, and economic practices relating to the production and consumption of food. Cereals (such as rice, millet, and sorghum), yams, black-eyed peas, sesame (benne), muskmelons, okra, and Guinea squash were subsistence crops transferred from Africa to Carolina. Slave-ship captains relied on these African staples to keep their enslaved cargo alive during the Middle Passage.[3] Just as Africans formed a diaspora throughout the Lowcountry topography, so did the "shadow world of cultivation" that represented African subsistence diets. Rice was just one of many staples transferred through the Middle Passage that appeared in the gardens of African slaves (Carney and Rosomoff 2009).

The close connection of African slaves to Lowcountry wetlands and small-stream floodplains provided access for subsistence agriculture. The proximity of plantation settlement highlands and low-lying wetlands enabled 17th-century slaves to construct nearby rice fields "on the plantation periphery" (Carney and Rosomoff 2009, Price 1991). Early plantation settlement patterns consisted of the plantation owner and enslaved houses close together on highland knolls or ridgelines. The Lowcountry topography's highland swells—caused by Pleistocene deposits and resulting erosion—created a landscape of high land surrounded by bays, streams, creeks, and rivers. For select West Africans transplanted in this New World environment, nearby wetlands provided similar spatial zones for growing rice. Relying on cultural memory, these enslaved cultivators constructed embankments where they could grow patches of rice in similar fashion to their homeland. Working away from the plantation settlements, slaves also noted potential sites when cutting cypress or herding cattle in swamps. As Peter Wood (1974) notes,

---

[3] The Middle Passage is defined as the middle leg of a three-part voyage trading cargo between Europe, Africa, and the New World. The second, or middle, leg of this trade route began with European traders exchanging iron, cloth, alcohol, firearms, and gunpowder in return for slaves. Ships departed central West African ports for the Americas, where the surviving slaves were exchanged for sugar, rice, tobacco, and other commodities.

these "black pioneers" were a mobile population that negotiated through a landscape often avoided by European-Americans. As part of the "numerous aspects of their varied African experience" in the Lowcountry, rice became one of many subsistence crops slaves grew upon the unwanted land (Edelson 2006a).

The appearance of rice in the subsistence fields of African slaves coincided with the age of experimentation by colonists, with prospective planters seeking out plants that would take root in the fertile soil for both subsistence and profit. By the late 17th century, English colonists were questioning how best to incorporate rice into their diet while also cultivating rice as an exportable crop. John Stewart (1931), for example, recommended substituting rice for barley to make beer and ale. South Carolinian colonists incorporated rice into their staple diet, first by subsidizing ground rice flour for wheat and corn to simulate England's "fine wheaten bread" unavailable in the New World. The grain also provided additional "fodder" for poultry and livestock. The versatility of rice as a food for both Africans and Europeans distinguished it from other plants grown for consumption and profit (Edelson 2006a).

Reservoir Rice Cultivation

Once European colonists recognized the importance of impounded water to simultaneously irrigate the rice crop and eradicate competing vegetation, a dramatic shift in landscape perceptions and activity occurred from the upland and savannah ecosystems down to the cypress-hardwood stream systems (fig. 2). Colonists looked beyond the "wasteland" to see unlimited potential in transforming the low-lying small-stream floodplains into orderly agricultural zones. The flow of water through wetlands fed the dense vegetation that added to the apparent "inexhaustible fertility" of the South Carolina Lowcountry (Anonymous 1845). Colonial naturalist Mark Catesby (1977) noted that inland swamps similar to the Huger Creek watershed were "impregnated by the washings from the higher lands, in a series of years are become vastly rich, and deep of soyl [sic] consisting of a sandy loam of a dark brown colour." One rice planter described inland swamps having a "better foundation and soil than any other lands" and "by nature more durable" for cultivation because of rainfall running down-stream "fine supplies of decayed vegetable, which are deposited while the waters are passing over said lands" (Anonymous 1828).

Soil that provided a foundation for these plantations varied in material, from sandy soils in higher well-drained pine-barrens down to less permeable loam and clay in low-lying wetlands. Although inland fields were localized in distinct watersheds, the microenvironments used for inland rice cultivation contained the same soil features. Meggett loam was the soil series often associated with inland rice zones. The Meggett series had a mixture, or a loam, of sand, clay, silt, and organic matter (Latimber 1916, Long 1980).

The slow water permeability and high water-holding capacity of Meggett loam were two characteristics that benefited inland rice cultivation. Slow water permeability means that the soil content prevents water from efficiently

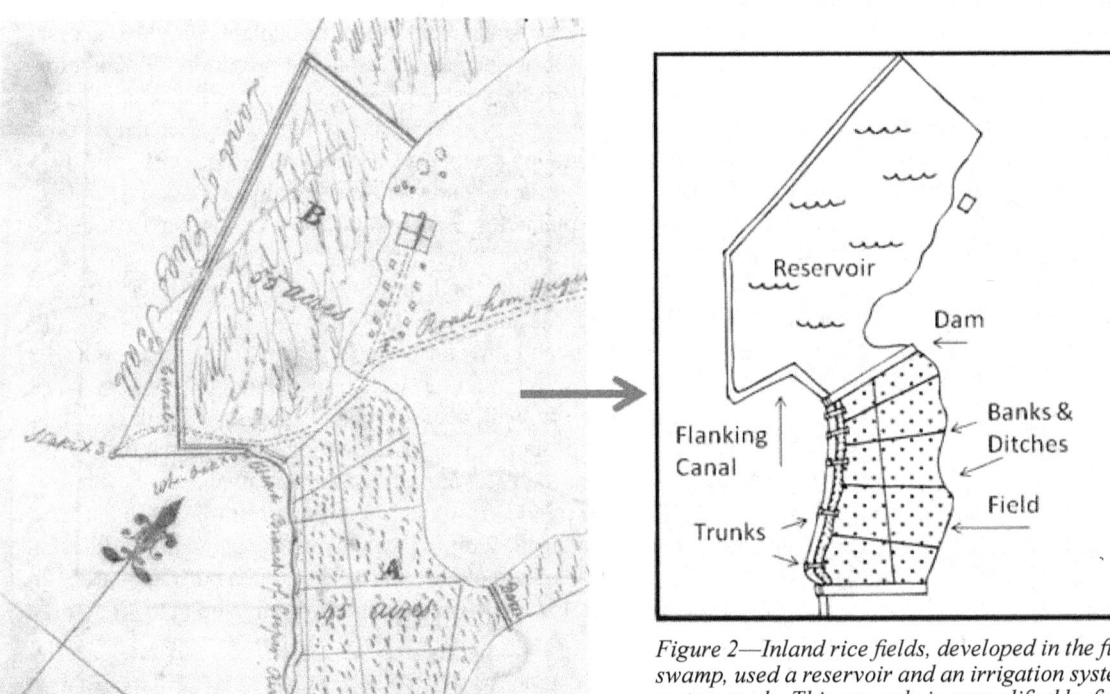

Figure 2—Inland rice fields, developed in the floodplain swamp, used a reservoir and an irrigation system to regulate water supply. This example is exemplified by fields illustrated from a 1790 Windsor Plantation plat (detail). [Plat of Windsor Plantation (detail) courtesy of the Charleston County Register Mesne Conveyance, Charleston, SC; Book: D6, page: 199. Schematic of the inland rice fields drawn by Lillian Trettin.]

draining through the ground. This feature allowed rice cultivators to effectively retain water in the reservoirs and the fields. Because of their low water permeability, soil from these zones was also used to construct the embankments. By reinforcing the retaining walls with clay, slaves created a basin to hold water within the natural terrain. South Carolina Governor James Glen (1761) wrote that "the best land for rice is a wet, deep, miry soil; such as is generally to be found in Cypress Swamps; or a black greasy Mould with a Clay Foundation; but the very best lands may be meliorated by laying them under water at proper Seasons." However, the compacted soil that created desirable conditions for retaining water also provided hardship for enslaved laborers shaping the landscape.

The ability to draw a steady amount of water was the second characteristic that planters needed to successfully cultivate inland rice. The Huger Creek topography provided planters and slaves consistent access to water for rice field irrigation. Unlike tidal rice cultivation, where planters and slaves harnessed the "estuary hydraulics" of the river's ebb and flow, inland planters relied on precipitation and water simply flowing from higher elevations down to the fields (Stewart 1996). These cultivators had to contain the natural resource from reliable surface and ground water sources—represented in drainage basins, swamps, bays, and springs. Watersheds composed of Meggett loam were relatively level, so water flow through these zones was a slow-moving current. Water flowing through these inland watersheds posed erosion problems only in extreme situations of flash floods, called freshets.

Colonial planters used enslaved West African labor to utilize water sources with the available land. The basic inland rice field consisted of two earthen dams enclosing a low-lying area bordered by ridges. Slaves built up the embankments with available fill from adjoining drainage trenches. The dam on higher elevation contained stream or spring fed water to form a reservoir, or a "reserve," that would provide a water supply to the lower rice fields. Once cultivators released water from the reservoir, a second dam retained this resource to irrigate rice plants and kill off competing vegetation. Located between these two earthen structures was a series of smaller embankments and ditches to channel and drain water effectively during the cultivation process (Hilliard 1975).

Water control for inland rice cultivation required not only precise construction of earthen embankments but also an understanding of the topography. Inland cultivators had to choose where reservoirs and fields would exist in relation to watercourses and terrain. To retain water in the reservoir and rice fields, the soil required a substantial clay foundation to prevent impounded water from seeping out. The subtle elevation change, in some cases just 3 or 4 feet from sandy highlands to alluvial swamps, allowed different types of vegetation to take root, depending upon the ground

permeability. This provided cultivators some insight into soil composition. For example, longleaf pine and oak communities grew in well drained sandy soil while cypress and tupelo gum communities grew in less permeable soil. To aspiring rice cultivators, who did not have access to the insights of soil science until the mid-19th century, the distribution of trees and other plants directed them toward appropriate inland sites.[4] The importance of water management explains why inland rice cultivators required "careful observance of topography and water flow" to properly retain and release water (Carney 1996).

Dense hardwoods, such as bald cypress (*Taxodium distichum*), tupelo gum (*Nyssa aquatica*), and sweet gum (*L. styraciflua)* were removed with axes and saws. Clearing the dense forests took an unimaginable amount of labor, and meant slashing and burning trees. Slaves cleared the colonial rice fields, first by burning underbrush, then by hoeing the weed roots to prevent recurring growth of competing vegetation. Field hands spent January and February, "down" months in the agricultural cycle, to burn existing rice fields or clear new acreage. Once vegetation was removed in South Carolina inland tracts, slaves had to level potential fields to prepare for rice planting and water drainage. After fields were developed to drain standing water, slaves constructed precise quarter ditches that removed floodwaters more effectively. Geometrically shaped fields eventually replaced the fluid landscape, redefining the nonhuman landforms of streams, banks, and knolls (Carney 2001, Clifton 1978, Littlefield 1981).

Rice cultivators used gates, or "trunks," to control waterflow from reservoirs onto the rice fields. Originally made from hollowed out trees, trunks were traditional African devices to regulate waterflow through a conduit by plugging the end of *Brassus* palms. Slaves substituted cypress for this device. Field engineers placed trunks in sloughs, or stream channels, so water ran efficiently out of the holding pond from the embankment's lowest point. Sloughs were an important natural feature for draining the wetlands, for they served as a "gutter" or a depression in the subtle elevation change. After these floodwaters nourished the soil and rice crop, and killed competing weeds, slaves drained the fields through trunks located at the second embankment. The water released from these fields flowed downhill toward nearby tidal rivers (Carney 2001, Doar 1936, Littlefield 1981).

Development of Limerick, Windsor, and Fishbrook during the first half of the 18th century represents the gradual transformation of these plantations into active inland rice environments and plantation settlements. From the first introduction of reservoir-irrigated rice to 1740, these

---

[4] Joyce Chaplin (1993) notes that, although soil sciences did not evolve until the mid-1800s, people developed a basic understanding of which soils were fertile and which soil did not allow proper drainage.

Inland rice field embankment in the Fox Gully floodplain. (Photo by Carl Trettin)

plantations developed basic inland rice cultivation systems. Daniel Huger (II) devoted 89 percent of Limerick's plantation capital to rice and livestock by his death in 1754. By 1724, Christopher Arthur devoted 24 slaves in maintaining 250 acres "which are now improved and cultivated" at the confluence of Nicholson and Turkey Creeks. In his will, Arthur does not specifically address rice cultivation, but he emphasizes that his heirs Patrick Roche and Bartholomew Arthur cultivate 150 and 100 acres, respectively, to "make fit to produce such Corn and Grain and other commodity as that country affords." Each heir received 12 people from Christopher Arthur's enslaved labor force, so a reduced enslaved population of could maintain limited acreage (Lees 1981).

Patrick Roche of Windsor Plantation ordered his enslaved laborers to sculpt fields out of the Nicholson Creek cypress bottomlands by 1725. Fishbrook Field, named after the neighboring plantation on Turkey Creek, was the result of cutting trees, removing cypress stumps, and shaping 45 acres of land. Nicholson Creek's meandering channel passed the Fishbrook Field's western border, separated by an earthen embankment. The Roches then diverted the creek away from the middle of the floodplain by embanking a 55-acre division and channeling water into

a flanking canal. Unlike Fishbrook Field, the second field division impeded the natural watercourse with an earthen dam and then redirected the creek around the western perimeter. A variation of this system consisted of two canals flanking the fields on each side. Duel canals increased efficiency of moving water around fields during freshets and also provided additional flexibility in flooding and draining individual divisions. Slightly higher elevation enabled planters to cultivate corn, peas, and indigo as additional provisional and economic crops (Anonymous 1784, Windsor Plantation [Plat]. 1790).

The second half of the 18th century represented an increase of the inland rice infrastructure. After a 21-year depression stemming from King George's War (1739-1748), the Stono Rebellion (1739), and yellow fever (1739, 1745, 1748, 1758) and smallpox (1738, 1758, 1760) epidemics, the South Carolina rice market again began an upward economic and manufacturing cycle in 1760. A combination of internal and international factors advanced rice prices in the second half of the 18th century, spurring an increase in Lowcountry rice production. Shipping increased between Europe and North America after the end of King George's War in 1748. European demand for rice grew dramatically after a series of poor grain harvests in late 1760s, motivating the British

Parliament to remove tariffs and import more of the South Carolina cash crop. These environmental hardships suffered by European grain producers, and changing trade practices, led to a 50 percent increase in imports of Carolina rice between 1760 and 1775 (Hardy 2001, Nash 1992).

Robert Quash's acquisition of Fishbrook signifies the demand for inland swamps. Bartholomew Arthur sold his 1,880 acres to Quash and Robert Brown in 1735. Between 1735 and 1757, Quash methodically purchased three divisions to unify the original Arthur tract, plus he purchased an additional 154 wetland acres from Gabriel Manigault of Silk Hope. In this 32-year period, the property value increased from £5,000 to £5,756, reflecting the rising demand for spatial zones of rice cultivation (Quash 1763).

As rice planters learned more about water control, they become more motivated to increase their rice acreage. Their new understanding led to new methods of drawing water onto and off of the rice fields. Windsor Plantation demonstrates how flanking canals—waterways that bordered the rice fields—took shape. Windsor's fields fit within the tight boundary of the Nicholson Creek floodplain. The elevation difference between pineland communities and the cypress hardwood forest varied between 30 and 40 feet within 1,000 feet, as the geological "unconformities" of the Bethera Scarp allowed Nicholson Creek to gorge out steeper "landscape gradients" compared to the Penholoway and Queen Anne Terraces (Colquhoun 1969). The watershed has a dramatic elevation change compared to the 5- to 10-foot elevation decline in the same 1,000-foot increment along the Cooper River tidal floodplains. Through the 18th century, the Roche family optimistically surveyed four divisions within the confines of the scarp to the northwest and the Talbot plain highlands to the southeast. Yet Ebenezer Roche had only one division of 45 acres developed for rice cultivation, with 24 "mostly country born" people under his control by 1783. The Roches relied on the predominant knoll forming Nicholson Creek's southern boundary to contain the inland rice fields. Forming a crescent shape around a 40-foot bluff, Nicholson Creek connected with Turkey Creek to form Huger Creek and serve as the headwaters of the Eastern Branch of the Cooper River. This bluff served as an optimal site for the Windsor house, slave settlement, and outbuildings (Anonymous 1784, Irving 1840-1852).

The American Revolution served as a major division point for cultural, economic, and political events in the Carolina Lowcountry. While only isolated skirmishes took place throughout the Cooper River watershed, the outcome would have lasting effects on all inhabitants. Much of the plantation infrastructure was left to ruin, with 7 years of warfare leaving untended rice fields destroyed or overgrown. Freshets eroded reservoir dams and field embankments, while volunteer, or wild, rice overtook uncultivated plots. Enslaved African-Americans also saw opportunity to leave plantations, leaving a limited labor force to continue cultivating rice. However, agricultural change rippled through the early republic period. Lowcountry planters sought more capital to reinvest in their neglected plantations. As a result of new opportunities, many planters replaced inland for tidal rice and indigo for cotton (Chaplin 1993, Morgan 1998).

Rice and Cotton in the Antebellum Landscape

Tidal Rice Cultivation

The antebellum period saw the dominance of a second type of rice plantation. Tidal cultivation, although closer to inland fields, relied on different topographic and hydrologic settings. Tidal cultivation used hydrology governed by the tidal cycle of the ocean, with a falling tide, or ebb, and a rising tide, or flow, to capture the energy of freshwater rivers for irrigating or draining the rice fields (fig. 3). Permanent embankments and surrounding interior ditches kept high water out of fields and floodwater in, and allowed proper draining of fields. Like inland fields, rice trunks controlled water flowing in and out of the embankments, yet these wooden devices were modified to allow a multidirectional flow of water. To achieve this, planters designed gates to cover both ends of the trunk. When fields needed flooding, slaves would open the exterior gate closest to the river, while the interior gate pivoted on a hinge for water to flow naturally into fields from the force of the tide. Once the tide changed direction, slaves closed both gates to prevent impounded water from leaving the fields. After the desired time elapsed for irrigating the fields, slaves raised the interior gate to allow water to flow out of the pivoted exterior gate, preventing resurgent tidal waters from flowing into the fields. Tidal rice fields were subdivided into smaller plots to efficiently control waterflow. By building levies on a grid system, planters could direct waterflow more precisely. These embankments were called quarter divisions because they were originally a quarter of an acre. Planters connected these divisions to a network of canals, ditches, and drains to properly irrigate the crop (Hilliard 1975, Stewart 1991).

Although tidal rice cultivation was used in the Colonial period, the irrigation practice rapidly expanded after the Revolution. Planters had to reinvest capital to repair their rice fields after the war, so many chose to focus on the new tidal technology. Because of the dramatic shift from inland to tidal cultivation, there was an agricultural movement from inland swamps to freshwater marshes (fig. 4). This location adjacent to tidal rivers provided more effective transportation and incorporation of tidal powered threshing mills and processing capabilities with higher output. By 1795, Elias Ball, Jr., commissioned Jonathan Lucas to design a water-powered mill that would grind the husks off rice.

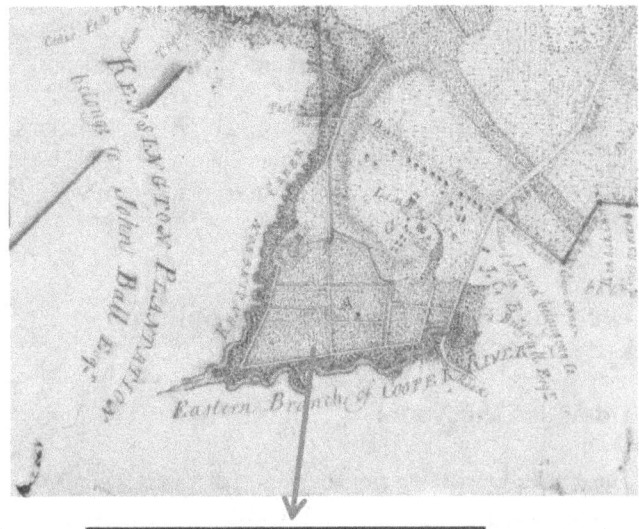

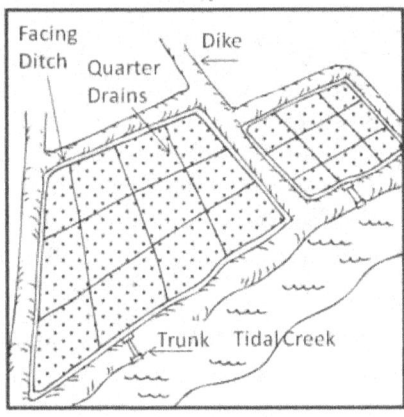

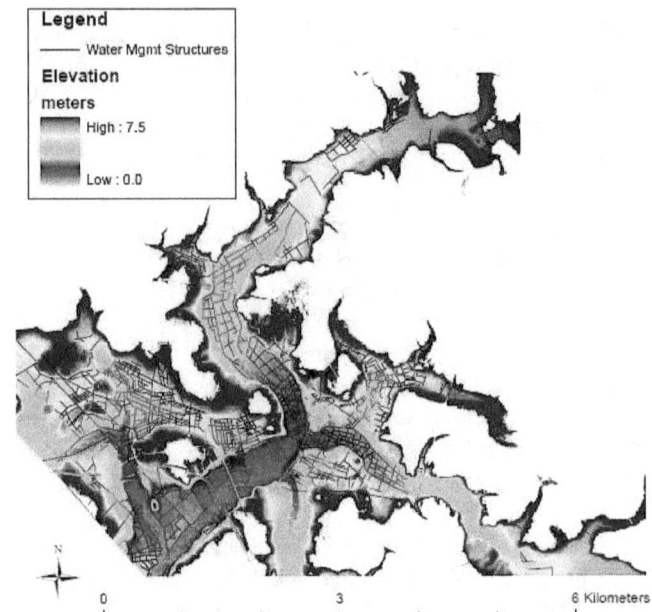

The mill sat along a canal leading from Limerick's inland fields to Kensington Creek, ultimately feeding into the East Branch of the Cooper River. Limerick was also the only plantation within the Santee Experimental Forest to actively produce tidal irrigated rice. Ball's enslaved laborers planted 125 acres of rice in 1790, yet had cleared, diked, and drained 335 acres for cultivation by 1797 (Lees 1981).

With the rise of tidal rice cultivation, planters reaped more wealth compared to their inland predecessors. They also produced a new variety of rice, called "Carolina Gold" because of the gold sheath, not the grain, which reflected a higher quality or premium rice. It appeared on the market in the late 18th century, just as tidal cultivation was taking hold in the Lowcountry. An advantage of this variety was its high yields and easily milled hull, which made it more efficient to process and market, compared to earlier inland white grain. Rice output exploded in 1800, for example, with 28,500 tons of rice was exported from rice producing States, principally South Carolina and Georgia. By 1815, 41,350 tons were exported, and in 1828 exports rose to 51,500 tons. Eventually, the national exports peaked in 1835, with 64,000 tons. Carolina Gold's higher grain quality resulted

in a greater demand from rice factors, promoting a higher price on the international exchange market after the Revolution and establishing this cash crop as a central commodity on the international market (Gray 1933).

Limerick's rice output reflected the changing antebellum cultivation strategies. Ball cultivated 121 acres in 1810, 4 acres less compared to 20 years prior. Acreage steadily grew between 1810 and 1815, totaling 181 acres. However, Ball's agricultural strategy dramatically decreased his cultivated rice acreage. Ball rotated corn and cotton on Limerick's Nicholson Creek rice fields during this period, cultivating only 39 acres in 1816 and 37 acres in 1817. Beginning in 1818, Ball increased his rice acres, devoting over 80 acres to "river swamp" rice cultivation. Although tidal irrigation technology was practiced on the Cooper River, and Ball had embanked rice fields bounding the East Branch, before the Revolution, no mention of Limerick tidal irrigation occurred before the 19th century. According to available records, Ball steadily devoted more acreage between 1820 and 1825, maximizing his output at Limerick in 1823 to 154 acres (Ball 1631-1895, Ball 1746-1999).

A typical rice field in the latter half of the 19th century. The rice fields were developed in bottomland hardwood forests, visible behind the fields. (Source: Robert N. Dennis collection of stereoscopic views of South Carolina. http://commons.wikimedia.org/wiki/File:Rice_field,_South_Carolina,_from_Robert_N._Dennis_collection_of_ stereoscopic_views.png. Prepared by Lee Moreland)

Long-Staple Cotton

Isaac Ball began planting black-seed, long-staple cotton at Limerick in 1810. Although planters introduced black-seed cotton (*Gossypium barbadense*) from the West Indies to the Atlantic Coast before 1785, shifts in the political economy for the high-quality, fine, long-staple variety motivated Lowcountry planters to devote more capital and labor to the cash crop after the Revolution. Coastal planters cultivated the black-seed variety into the celebrated Sea Island cotton during the Antebellum period. However, inland planters could not recreate the variety's desired filament due to subtle environmental conditions, cross-pollination with green-seed (short-staple) cotton, and poor seed selection. As a result, cotton factors separated the black-seed variety into three market classes: Sea Island, Santee long, and Mains (Porcher and Fick 2005).

While long-staple cotton became a mainstay in St. John's Parish during the antebellum period, Limerick's cotton production was inconsistent. Ball originally devoted 5½ acres to growing black-seed cotton in 1810. Seven years later, Ball expanded to 100 acres, rotating his workforce of enslaved laborers among the rice, cotton, and corn fields. Production continued to 1824 but ceased on Limerick by the 1850 census. Both Windsor and Fishbrook employed similar agricultural practices, growing cotton in marginal quantities, while labor was primarily devoted to rice and corn. By the eve of the Civil War, Limerick was producing 558,830 pounds of rice. Also diversifying the Ball crop was sweet potatoes, corn, peas, and beans, as well as butter making, establishing the cash value of the plantation at $40,000 (Ball 1631-1895, Lees 1981, Porcher and Fick 2005).

One reason for the limited cotton production came from the environmental conditions. Black-seed cotton required well-drained sandy soil. This variety could not tolerate a saturated soil because water prevented adequate oxygen intake from the roots. High land in the Huger Creek watershed Wahee-Duplin-Lenoir association consisted of somewhat poorly drained loamy surface with a high water table. Soil conditions suitable for rice cultivation did not complement cotton agriculture. Although the upland soils were moderately well drained sandy loam, the clay loam subsoil restricted adequate drainage. To work within these environmental limitations, the planters constructed raised beds, or ridges, between 18 inches to 2 feet in height that helped create soil permeability. Drainage ditches between the raised beds also helped direct standing water away from the cotton roots down to the low-lying flood plains (Long 1980, Porcher and Fick 2005).

Postbellum Agricultural Changes

Rice, Cotton, and Truck Farming

The lasting results of the Civil War came from the emancipation of enslaved labor and the demise of the plantation system. The removal of slave labor led to a restructuring of economic and social patterns, with agricultural endeavors suffering a slow demise in the Lowcountry. African-Americans could migrate freely, which created a shift in the labor populations of rural communities, as many sought employment in urban centers or other rural communities. The two most successful cash crops in the antebellum Lowcountry, rice and cotton, did not disappear overnight. Instead, agricultural landscapes shifted over time as landowners failed to turn profits, faced competing new technologies, and succumbed to natural disasters.

Huger Creek planters struggled to maintain economic security from rice culture after the Civil War. Rice output on Limerick dropped from 558,830 pounds in 1860 to 2,000 pounds 10 years later. William J. Ball recovered by bringing the output up to 24,000 pounds in 1880, but the economic success did not compare to before the Civil War. The Gibbs family did not fare much better at Windsor. John C. Gibbs managed Windsor for his mother, but the family sold the property in tracts, purchased by land speculator Charles Greenland McCay in 1878 and Ada Guilds in 1886. The postbellum period represented economic diversity once again on Limerick, Windsor, and Fishbrook. With the collapse of the rice culture, Huger Creek planters sought income from cattle ranching, cotton, corn, and peas (Lees 1981).

Limerick Plantation, 1916. Note: Live Oak drive in foreground. (Photo by W.B. Barrows. Photo courtesy of the Forest History Society, Durham, NC; USFS negative number 26336A.)

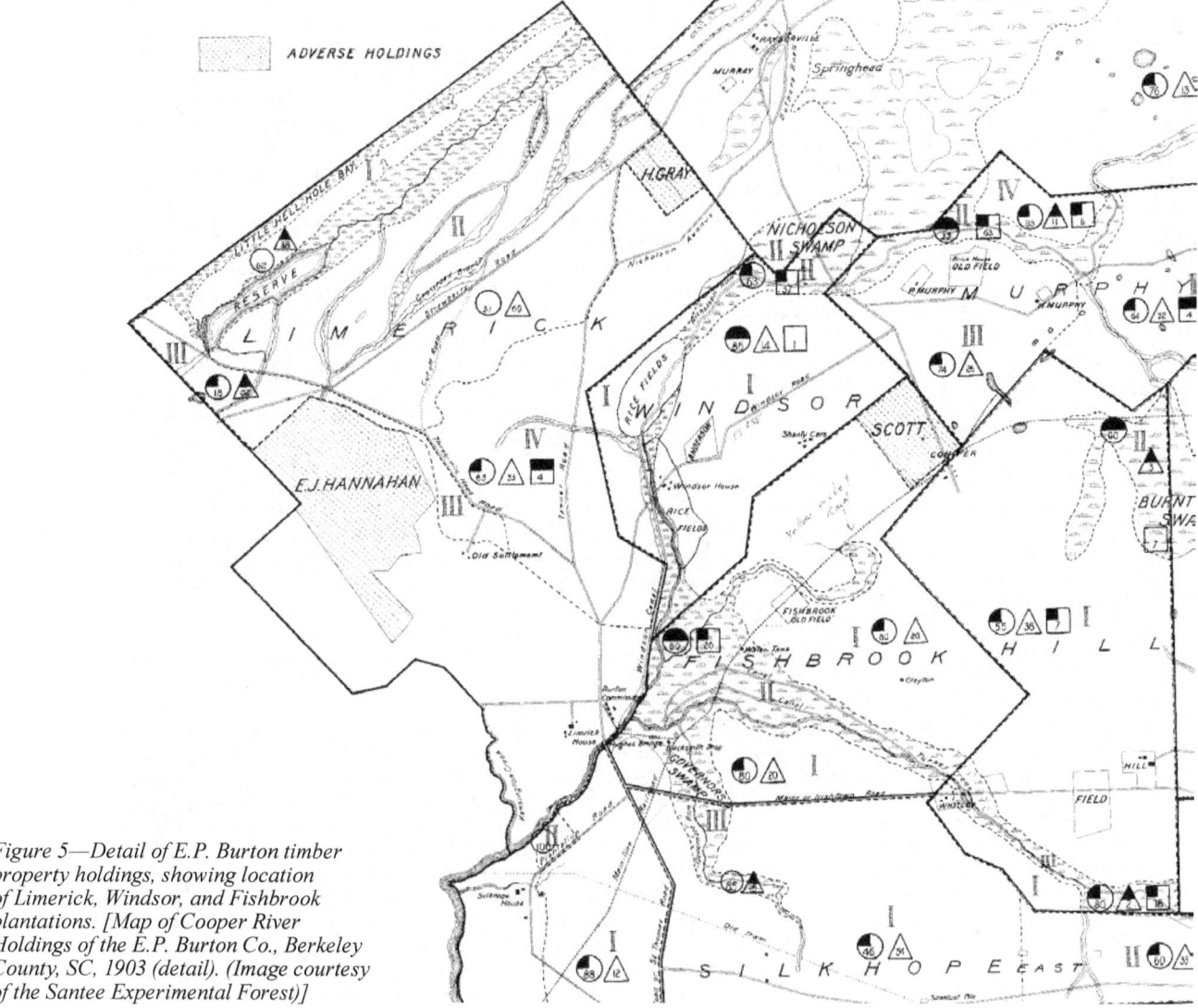

Figure 5—Detail of E.P. Burton timber property holdings, showing location of Limerick, Windsor, and Fishbrook plantations. [Map of Cooper River Holdings of the E.P. Burton Co., Berkeley County, SC, 1903 (detail). (Image courtesy of the Santee Experimental Forest)]

Emancipated slaves living on these properties originally made agreements with the Ball and Gibbs families to establish working conditions after the war. Twenty-one people signed a contract with J.C. Gibbs to work on the Windsor fields and reside on the property. W.J. Ball expressed frustration from the lack of output from his former slaves, stating that the work was inferior compared to the "old system." Field hands received one-third of the total crop, which was customary during the Reconstruction period (Ball 1631-1895).

The rise of vegetable truck farming took the place of these cash crops immediately following the Civil War. Former plantation owners leased their land to sharecroppers, who grew agricultural products for sale in Charleston, SC, and Mt. Pleasant, SC. Crops such as potatoes, cabbage, beans, and cucumbers became economic commodities for the former slaves. African-Americans who chose to abandon cotton farming from the boll weevil epidemic or failure of the Lowcountry rice economy could still maintain economic subsistence through agricultural practice (Latimber 1916, Murray 1949).

Timber Industry

Residents of 20th-century South Carolina, like their predecessors, were forced to make new decisions for economic survival. Although naval stores continued in one form or another since the Colonial period, a more industrial method of tapping into the timber resources took place during the postbellum period. During the late 19th and early 20th centuries, individual property owners began selling their plantations to lumber companies. By 1906, E.P. Burton Lumber Company purchased Limerick, Windsor, Fishbrook, and surrounding plantations to amass 47,000 acres (fig. 5). They changed the landscape by building an infrastructure of railroads, causeways, and logging camps for quickly extracting upland timber, and as a consequence, within 15 years, they left a clear-cut environment (Hester 1997).

E.P. Burton's expanding infrastructure across the landscape reflected the company's growing logging operations in the Huger Creek watershed. Between 1899 and 1902, the timber company operated a commissary, employee housing, and a blacksmith shop next to Huger

ABOVE: *Forested old rice field in the floodplain of Fox Gully creek on the Santee Experimental Forest. (Photo by author.)*
RIGHT: *Hardwood logs at lumber mill next to railroad tracks, Berkeley County, SC. [Photo by Arthur Bernard Recknagel. Photo courtesy of the Forest History Society, Durham, NC; Arthur Bernard Recknagel Photograph Collection (Reck2_25A).]*

bridge. The village catered to the initial stages at Limerick and was connected to Burton's railroad by a spur branch. As E.P. Burton expanded into Windsor and Fishbrook, the company built a second village in 1902. Located approximately 5 miles from the Burton dock at Silk Hope on the East Branch of the Cooper, Conifer originally consisted of employee housing and cook's quarters. In 4 years, the village grew to 500 people and supported a blacksmith's shop, a commissary, a superintendent's office, a doctor's office, and a company house to lodge the foresters.[5]

By 1906, Burton railroads crossed 11 miles of the Santee Experimental Forest. Under ideal conditions, employees could lay up to 150 yards of ties and rails a day. However, the varied terrain presented challenges building log trestles and earthen causeways over the wetlands. Burton engineers either reinforced former rice embankments or constructed new earthworks to support the locomotives and cars encroaching into the forest lands (Chapman 1905, Fetters 1990).

This form of industrialization was part of a larger trend across the United States. Logging activity within the Huger Creek watershed was a result of new technologies to extract timber, such as band saws and skidders, combined with the increased demand for wood products from the boom of industrial growth in the South. Still reeling from the economic collapse after the Civil War, Charleston and its port depended upon the growing logging industry in the Huger Creek watershed. By 1913, three Charleston-area timber companies had a cumulative annual production of over 300 million board feet (Hester 1997).

---

[5] Now located at the crossroads of Conifer and Yellow Jacket Road.

Federal Land Aquisition

Forest Conservation

The Federal Government's 1928 approval of the Wambaw Purchase Unit represents a broader trend of the rapid pace of industrialism in forested landscapes. As a result of timber companies rapidly depleting forests throughout the Eastern United States, a new concept handling the nonhuman landscape evolved to become conservation. Gifford Pinchot, a leader of the conservation movement, saw people as stewards of the land but also believed that nature is meaningful only when it serves multiple and practical human purposes. To Pinchot, forestry was both an art and a science. He believed that industrial logging could safely continue with the expertise of scientifically trained professionals. Pinchot carried this ideology with him to the newly created United States Division of Forestry, where he became chief forester in 1898. Two years later, he helped created the Yale Forestry School, the Nation's premier forestry education and research institution. Pinchot's conservation success was reflected in the area of land managed by the Division of Forestry, which grew during Theodore Roosevelt's time as president of the United States (1901-1910)—from 51 million acres to 175 million (Miller 2001).

To Pinchot, sustained yield of timber and cooperation between the government and landowners was a duel concept system for properly managing forest lands. The first concept, sustained yield of timber, embraced a businesslike philosophy that purported that capital, which produced annual growth resulting in interest, lay in managing healthy timber stands. By practicing sustained yields, timber companies would harvest the interest, or the annual growth, of the forest. The second concept, cooperation between the government and landowners, stressed that the Division of Forestry educate private landholders on successful forestry practices. The Division of Forestry consulted timber companies on how to manage sustainable timber stands. In return, the Division of Forestry put their scientific management to use with real-world scenarios (Miller 2001).

As part of this cooperative effort, forestry assistant Charles S. Chapman and five assistants worked with E.P. Burton from December 1902 to March 1903, studying the health of the forest on the Huger Creek watershed. Chapman's 1905 report provided a snapshot into forestry practices and landscape alteration at the time. Chapman stressed the importance of healthy growth and harvesting practices of the loblolly pine stands, representing 34 percent of forested E.P. Burton land. Loblolly became the dominant species on abandoned upland fields, replacing cotton, corn, and peas. Loblolly also became the dominant species after a clear-cut of longleaf stands. Recognizing the economic benefit of loblolly, "being a tree of very rapid growth and being well suited to the locality," Chapman advised E.P. Burton to remove the threat of fire to the species, protect immature pines acting as seed trees, and cut only trees with a diameter of 14 inches or greater (Chapman 1905).

At the same time, Yale students affiliated with the Forest Service, U.S. Department of Agriculture, began working with E.P. Burton between 1902 and 1906 on the Limerick Plantation Tract. In 1928, A.B. Recknagel and the Cornell School of Forestry conducted research on Limerick, Windsor, and Fishbrook. This property became early platforms for the development of North American silviculture, a precursor to the mission of the Santee Experimental Forest (Hester 1997, Recknagel 1928).

The Santee Experimental Forest

The Santee Experimental Forest originated from a series of initiatives addressing the complexity of forest land use and management. Henry S. Graves, Pinchot's

Hardwood stand in Huger Creek watershed. Cornell College of Forestry students at base of the tree. [Photo by Arthur Bernard Recknagel. Photo courtesy of the Forest History Society, Durham, NC; Arthur Bernard Recknagel Photograph Collection (Reck2_9A).]

handpicked successor as chief forester, established the Branch of Research in 1915 to manage research activities of the Forest Experiment Stations, the Forest Products Laboratory, and the Washington Offices of Products and Silviculture. In 1921, the Branch of Research created the Appalachian Forest Experiment Station in Asheville, NC. This experiment station would eventually supervise the Santee Experimental Forest in South Carolina. By the second decade of the 20th century, a compilation of Federal and State conservation policies helped protect land. On the Federal level, a gradual movement of Forest Service officials recognized that cooperation with individual landowners and timber companies could not solve universal deforestation and land mismanagement. Instead, the Forest Service took steps to solve the land problem through direct Federal land acquisition and land management. The Clarke-McNary Act of 1924 resulted from this philosophy, where the legislature granted the Federal Government permission to acquire lands specifically for timber production plus providing forest protection funds to States that had established forestry departments. On the State level, boosters' lobbing efforts successfully led to the creation of the State Forestry Commission in 1927. The establishment of the State Forestry Commission represented the growing statewide conservation network and provided resources for landowners to prevent forest fires and carry out reforestation principles. With the creation of this forestry department, South Carolina qualified for Clarke-McNary Act funding and also served as a State mediator between the Federal Government and private landowners (Hester 1997, Miller 2001, Paxton 1950) .

Forest Service officials who formed connections with timber companies and local politicians at the turn of the century deemed the Huger Creek watershed a model for restoration by 1927. E.P. Burton deforested their Huger Creek tract by 1916, with Dorchester and Tuxbury conducting a second cut by 1924. Timber companies cut over Limerick, Windsor, and Fishbrook Plantations to such an extent that land reformers viewed this spatial boundary as an ideal location to promote idealism that scientific forestry management could solve larger land problems occurring through the Southeastern Coastal Plain. The newly created State Forestry Commission served as a mediator between the Forest Service and the timber industry, while State and Federal agencies began identifying purchase units in 1927. The National Forest Reservation Commission established the Wambaw purchase unit in February 1928, yet 5 years passed before New Deal stimulus enabled the Forest Service to purchase individual tracts. Between 1933 and 1935, the Forest Service secured 195,000 acres, approximately 80 percent within the current Francis Marion boundary. On July 10, 1936, U.S. President Franklin D. Roosevelt proclaimed the former Wambaw unit the Francis Marion National Forest (Hester 1997, Paxton 1950).

With the Francis Marion National Forest secured, C.E. Rachford, Chief Forester, on July 6, 1937, signed "An Order Establishing the Santee Experimental Forest out of Certain Lands within the Francis Marion National Forest, South Carolina." The stated purpose of the Santee Experimental Forest was to "make permanently available for forest research and demonstration of its results" under the direction of the Appalachian Forest Experiment Station in subjects relating to "rate of growth, silvics and silviculture, and fire damage in the loblolly pine types of the Mid-Atlantic Coastal Province." Originally encompassing 5,000 acres overlaying Nicholson and Turkey Creeks, the Santee Experimental Forest expanded by 1,000 acres of Bethera Scarp highlands to the north and northeast on July 26, 1946. The 6,100-acre spatial landscape provided importance for the U.S. Department of Agriculture, as the area represented "forest conditions typical of the loblolly pine, loblolly pine-hardwoods, bottomland hardwoods, and loblolly pine-longleaf pine types in the Coastal Plain region of South Carolina" with "excellent opportunities" for the Forest Service to conduct improvement and protection of land with a wide history of land use. The Forest Service recognized the area's exhaustive land use, leaving a variety of forest growth from "young reproduction stands" to "severely cut and mistreated stands," presenting "desirable" conditions for silviculture experimentation representative of the Southern Coastal Plain (USDA 1966).

Literatue Cited

Anon. 1784. Inventory of Ebenezer Roche, 3 July. South Carolina Estate Inventories, A: 378. Columbia, SC: South Carolina Department of Archives and History.

Anon. 1828. Observations on the Winter Flowing of Rice Lands, in Reply to Mr. Munnerlyn's Answers to Queries, &c. by a Rice Planter. Southern Agriculturalist and Register of Rural Affairs. December; 1(12): 531.

Anon. 1854. Reclamation of Southern Swamps. DeBow's Review and Industrial Resources. November; 17(5): 525.

Ball Family Papers, 1631-1895. 52 microfiches. Charleston, SC: South Carolina Historical Society.

Ball Family Papers, 1746-1999. 51 microfiches. Columbia, SC: University of South Carolina, South Caroliniana Library.

Carney, J.A. 1996. Landscapes of Technology Transfer: Rice Cultivation and African Continuities. Technology and Culture. 37: 5-35.

Carney, J.A. 2001. Black Rice: The African Origins of Rice Cultivation in the Americas. Cambridge: Harvard University Press. 256 p.

Carney, J.A.; Rosomoff, R.N. 2009. In the Shadow of Slavery: Africa's Botanical Legacy in the Atlantic World. Berkeley: University of California Press. 296 p.

Catesby, M. 1977. Mark Catesby's Natural History, 1731-47. In: Merrins, H.R. ed. The Colonial South Carolina Scene: Contemporary Views, 1697-1774. Tricentenial Edition, number 7. Columbia, SC: University of South Carolina Press: 85-109.

Chaplin, J.E. 1993. An Anxious Pursuit: Agricultural Innovation and Modernity in the Lower South, 1730-1815. Chapel Hill: University of North Carolina Press. 430 p.

Chapman, C.S. 1905. A Working Plan for Forest Lands in Berkeley County, South Carolina. Bulletin 56. Washington, DC: U.S. Department of Agriculture, Bureau of Forestry. 62 p. + map.

Clifton, J.M., ed. 1978. Life and Labor on Argyle Island: Letters and Documents of a Savannah Rice Plantation, 1833-1867. Savannah: Beehive Press. 365 p.

Colquhoun, D.J. 1969. Geomorphology of the Lower Coastal Plain of South Carolina. Columbia: Division of Geology. 36 p.

Doar, D. 1936. Rice and Rice Planting in the South Carolina Lowcountry. Charleston: Charleston Museum. 70 p.

Dunn, R.S. 1972. Sugar and Slaves: The Rise of the Planter Class in the English West Indies, 1624-1713. Chapel Hill: The University of North Carolina Press. 379 p.

Edelson, S.M. 2006a. Plantation Enterprise: Plantation Enterprise in Colonial South Carolina. Cambridge: Harvard University Press. 400 p.

Edelson, S.M. 2006b. The Nature of Slavery: Environmental Disorder and Slave Agency in Colonial South Carolina. In: Olwell, R.; Tully, A., eds. Cultures and Identities in Colonial British America. Baltimore: Johns Hopkins University Press: 21-44.

Fetters, T. 1990. Logging Railroads of South Carolina. Forest Park, Il: Heimburger House Publishing Co. 266 p.

Glen, J. 1761. A Description of South Carolina: Containing Many Curious and Interesting Particulars Relating to the Civil, Natural and Commercial History of That Colony. London: R&J Dodsley. 116 p.

Gray, L.C. 1933. History of Agriculture in the Southern United States to 1860, 2 vols. Washington, DC: Carnegie Institution of Washington. 1086 p.

Hardy, S.G. 2001. Colonial South Carolina's Rice Industry and Atlantic Economy: Patterns of Trade, Shipping, and Growth, 1715-1775. In: Greene, J.P.; Brana-Shute, R.; Sparks, R.J., eds. Money, Trade, and Power: The Evolution of Colonial South Carolina's Plantation Society. Columbia: University of South Carolina Press: 108-140.

Hart, L.P. 1986. Excavations at the Limerick Tar Kiln Site (38BK472). Francis Marion and Sumter National Forests Cultural Resources Management Report, 86-52. Columbia: U.S. Department of Agriculture Forest Service. 45 p.

Hester, A. 1997. From Sustained Yield to Sustaining Communities: The Establishment of Francis Marion National Forest in South Carolina, 1901-1936. [Place of publication unknown]: U.S. Department of Agriculture, Forest Service. 35 p. On file with: Francis Marion National Forest, 2421 Witherbee Road, Cordesville, SC 29434.

Hewatt, A. 1779. An Historical Account of the Rise and Progress of the Colonies of South Carolina and Georgia. London: Alexander Donaldson. 679 p. 2 vols.

Hilliard, S.B. 1975. Antebellum Tidewater Rice Culture: An Ingenious Adaptation to Nature. In: Walker, H.J., ed., Coastal Resources. Geoscience and Man 12. Baton Rouge: Louisiana State Press: 57-66.

Irving, J.B. 1840-1852. Record of Windsor and Kensington Plantations. Charleston, SC: Charleston Library Society. 187 p.

Latimber, W.J. 1916. Soil Survey of Berkeley County, South Carolina. In: Whitney, M., ed. Field Operations of the Bureau of Soils, 1916. Washington, DC: U.S. Department of Agriculture, Bureau of Soils: 483-520.

Lees, W.B. 1981. The Historical Development of Limerick Plantation, a Tidewater Rice Plantation in Berkeley County, South Carolina, 1683-1945. South Carolina Historical Magazine. 82: 44-62.

Littlefield, D.C. 1981. Rice and Slaves: Ethnicity and the Slave Trade in Colonial South Carolina. Urbana: University of Illinois Press. 216 p.

Long, B.M. 1980. Soil Survey of Berkeley County, South Carolina. Washington, DC: U.S. Department of Agriculture, Soil Conservation Service and Forest Service. 102 p. + maps.

Miller, C. 2001. Gifford Pinchot and the Making of Modern Environmentalism. Washington, DC: Island Press. 384 p.

Morgan, P.D. 1998. Slave Counterpoint: Black Culture in the Eighteenth-Century Chesapeake and Lowcountry. Chapel Hill: University of North Carolina Press. 736 p.

Murray, C.S. 1949. This is Our Land: The Story of the Agricultural Society of South Carolina. Charleston: Carolina Art Association. 290 p.

Nash, R.C. 1992. South Carolina and the Atlantic Economy in the Late Seventeenth and Eighteenth Centuries. The Economic History Review, New Series 45: 677-702.

Otto, J.S. 1987. Livestock-Raising in Early South Carolina, 1670-1700: Prelude to the Early Rice Plantation Economy. Agricultural History. 61: 13-24.

Paxton, P.J. 1950. The National Forests and Purchase Units of Region Eight. Atlanta: U.S. Department of Agriculture Forest Service. 56 p.

Porcher, R.D. [In press]. The Market Preparation of Carolina Rice. Columbia: The University of South Carolina Press.

Porcher, R.D.; Fick, S. 2005. The Story of Sea Island Cotton. Charleston: Wyrick & Co. 577 p.

Price, R. 1991. Subsistence on the Plantation Periphery: Crops, Cooking, and Labour among Eighteenth-Century Suriname Maroons. Slavery and Abolition. 12: 107-127.

Pyne, S.J. 1997. Vestal Fire: An Environmental History, Told through Fire, of Europe and Europe's encounter with the World. Seattle: The University of Washington Press. 672 p.

Quash, R. 1763. Land Memorial. Columbia, SC: South Carolina Department of Archives and History. 6: 199.

Recknagel, A.B. 1928. Remeasuring the Hell Hole Plots in South Carolina. Journal of Forestry. 26: 823-824.

Smith, H.A.M. 1911. The Baronies of South Carolina: Cypress Barony. South Carolina Historical and Genealogical Magazine. 12: 5-13.

Stewart, J. 1931. Letters from John Stewart to William Dunlop. South Carolina Historical and Genelogical Magazine. 32: 1-33; 81-114; 170-174.

Stewart, M.A. 1991. Rice, Water, and Power: Landscapes of Domination and Resistance in the Lowcountry, 1790-1880. Environmental History Review. 15: 47-64.

Stewart, M.A. 1996. "What Nature Suffers to Groe:" Life, Labor, and Landscape on the Georgia Coast, 1680-1920. Athens: University of Georgia Press. 392 p.

U.S. Department of Agriculture, Forest Service. 1966. Establishment Report, April 12, 1937: An order establishing the Santee Experimental Forest out of certain lands within the Francis Marion National Forest, South Carolina, and Revision to Establishment Report by O. Gordon Langdon, June 20, 1966. Unpublished report. Charleston, SC: Southeastern Forest Experiment Station. Report available: Santee Experimental Forest, 3734 Hwy 402, Cordesville, SC 29434. 27 p. + map.

Ver Steeg, C.L. 1975. Origins of a Southern Mosaic: Studies of Early Carolina and Georgia. Athens: University of Georgia Press. 165 p.

Weir, R.M. 1997. Colonial South Carolina: A History. New York: KTO Press, 1983; Columbia: University of South Carolina Press. 430 p.

Windsor Plantation [Plat]. 1790. Book D7: 199. Charleston: Charleston County Register Mesne Conveyance.

Wood, P.H. 1974. Black Majority: Negroes in Colonial South Carolina from 1670 Through the Stono Rebellion. New York: A.A. Knopf. 370 p.

Smith, Hayden R. 2012 In Land of Cypress and Pine: An Environmental History of the Santee Experimental Forest, 1683-1937. Gen. Tech. Rep. SRS-155. Asheville, NC: U.S. Department of Agriculture Forest Service, Southern Research Station. 17 p.

Abstract—The Santee Experimental Forest is a 6,100-acre research facility located within the Francis Marion National Forest, SC. Situated within the Huger Creek watershed in the headwaters of the East Branch of the Cooper River, the Santee Experimental Forest supports research in forest ecology, silviculture, prescribed fire, forest hydrology, ecosystem restoration, and wildlife management. Although the Santee Experimental Forest came into existence based on early 20th-century timber practices and the resulting needs for information on sustainable forestry practices, its boundaries have supported a wide array of human development for over 300 years. This paper provides an overarching history of land use on the Forest and regional perspectives. This environmental history also explains how Huger Creek ecosystems influenced people's alteration the landscape. Livestock, naval stores, rice, cotton, and truck farming represent human production on the land from the colonial to postbellum eras. Logging and forest management replaced the earlier industries as political, social, and economic factors evolved at the turn of the 20th century. By documenting human development upon the land, a clear understanding of changing landscapes and ecological succession provides needed context for the Santee Experimental Forest's scope and mission. This environmental history also provides the basis for considering the influences of past uses on the delivery of ecosystem goods and services in a restored forest landscape.

Keywords: Environmental history, forest history, forest succession, Limerick Plantation, rice culture, Windsor Plantation.